THE EFFECT OF PLANNING AND CONTROL ON ORGANIZATIONAL PERFORMANCE.

(A STUDY OF 7UP BOTTLING COMPANY PLC, ABA)

BY

LUTHANS, F.

TABLE OF CONTENTS

CHAPTER ONE: INTRODUCTION

CHAPTER TWO: LITERATURE REVIEW

CHAPTER THREE: METHODOLOGY

CHAPTER FOUR: DATA PRESENTATION, ANALYSIS AND DISCUSSION OF FINDINGS

CHAPTER FIVE: SUMMARY OF FINDINGS, CONCLUSIONS AND RECOMMENDATIONS

LIST OF TABLES

LIST OF FIGURES

CHAPTER ONE

INTRODUCTION

1.1   Background of the Study

No organization can successfully exist without deciding in advance what the expected outcome or result is likely to be. The purpose and methods of attaining the said objectives and targets must be clearly stated. However, the purpose, methods of deciding well, in advance the target and objectives is a function of planning. People today indulge in so many activities without adequately considering them. Unfortunately, planning is one of these activities. One gets conscious of it sometimes when it really involves a very huge amount of money. Planning is not an event that stops suddenly. It is an ongoing process that reflects and adapts to changes in the environment.

According to Mcfarland (2001), planning involves thinking, anticipation and preparation of actions that will be carried out in order to achieve a specific goal or objective. It involves setting out step-by-step activities, which can lead to achievement of a set goal.

He also opined that planning is an activity by which the managers analyze present conditions to determine ways of reaching a desired future state. Therefore, it could be observed and understood that planning is futuristic. On the other hand, control is the practice of ensuring that the activities of firms conform to its plan, and that its objectives are achieved. In all organization, plans are made to obtain general objectives. The main purpose of managerial control is to ensure that planning or planned operations are carried out in such a way that the objectives will be met with success.

Pandy (2000), viewed that planning is diversified, noting that the importance is not only on profit making organization, but also on philanthropic, social clubs, religious organizations, military homes as well as individual activities. Many people ordinarily, engage in some operations without actually knowing that they are getting involved in management cadre and include all workers in the organization, especially where there are democratization or participation managerial practices.

According to Koontz (2001), planning is selecting from among alternative features, the course of action. For the enterprise and other departmental actions, effective managerial planning involves all decision making activities and the determination of how objectives are to be carried out. The manager should do this using these questions; Who will do the work? When will it be done? Planning is futuristic and therefore, can either be daily, Weekly, Monthly, Quarterly, Yearly or more than two years.

According to Mcfarland (2001), planning is an activity by which managers analyze present conditions to determine ways of reaching a desired future state. A good planning entails people involvement in making dreams to become reality. An effective business organization is an institution organized and operated to produce goods and services and cannot achieve results except there is efficient planning of the available resources.

Keriter (2008) defined planning as the process of coping with uncertainty by formulating results. Planning therefore, enables humans to achieve specified results by providing a partway from concept to reality. The greater the mission, the larger and more challenging the partway. Onuoha (2009) defined planning as the process of determining enterprises objectives and selecting future course of action necessary for their accomplishment.

Every organization strives towards Performance. It is the main goal. Organizational Performance is determined by a broad range of factors such as setting up of goals and objectives, the strategies, planning and controlling, etc. It is the capacity of an organization, institution or business to yield desired results with a minimum expenditure of energy, time, money, personnel, materials etc.

Performance is the lifeline of every organization, without which the organization is bound to fail. For an organization to be productive, it needs to consider these main factors; planning and controlling. Planning as a key to organization's performance involves selecting mission objectives and actions to achieve them. It bridges the gap from where we are to where we want to go. It can equally be analyzing a situation, determining the goals that will be pursued in the future, deciding in advance the actions that will be taken to achieve these goals.

Controlling enhances organizational performance by continuous monitoring of organization's progress and taking corrective actions, strategic planning, setting objectives and managing resources effectively. Planning and controlling as pertinent tools for ensuring organizational performance are very necessary. Therefore, a constant and comprehensive step in formulating strategic plans and putting in place certain appraisals and evaluating the system as a measure to control become necessary. The absence of planning and controlling limits the productive rate and growth of an organization.

1.2   Statement of the Research Problem

No doubt, proper planning and control is the main root of an effective organizational performance or performance in every establishment. When this inevitable aspect of production is not achieved, the overall aims and objectives of the organization can never be met. In other words, performance can be frustrated or sabotaged by the consequences of improper planning and control by top management and their subordinates.

Improper planning and control has led to the problems of poor industrial relationship between supervisors and subordinates, lack of interest and commitment on the part of workers in carrying out their respective duties effectively in many organizations in Nigeria.

Also, the attitude and response of management to workers' challenges and other issues have deprived employees of management's support, which often results to lack of job motivation. This problem has further created hidden cost to management, such as loss of goodwill and valuable employees.

The researcher therefore, bearing in mind the negative impact of improper planning and control in any organization, intends to find solutions to these problems, using 7Up Bottling Company PLC, Aba as case study.

1.3   Objectives of the Study

The general objective of the study is to find out the impact of planning and control on organizational performance in 7Up Bottling Company Plc, Aba. However, the specific objectives are:

1. To know the influence of contingency planning on organizational performance.
2. To ascertain the influence of tactical planning on organizational performance.
3. To know the influence of operational control on organizational performance.
4. To ascertain whether or not human and machine control influence organizational performance.

1.4   Research Questions

1. Does contingency planning influence organizational performance?
2. To what extent does tactical planning affect organizational performance?
3. What is the influence of operational control on organizational performance?
4. Does human and machine control influence organizational performance?

1.5   Research Hypotheses

Ho_1:   There is no significant relationship between contingency planning and organizational performance.

Ho_2:   There is no significant relational between tactical planning and organizational performance.

Ho_3:   There is no significant relationship between operational control and organizational performance.

Ho_4:   There is no significant relationship between human and machine control and organizational performance.

1.6   Scope of the Study

This study centres on the impact of planning and control on organizational performance, using 7Up Bottling Company PLC, Aba as case study. The reason for our choice is due to the fact that an organization at any level cannot be said to be productive without the necessary planning and control measures being put in place and properly followed to the letter.

Theoretical Scope: The theoretical Scope covers relevant literature on content theories of work motivation and process theories of work motivation. These include Maslow's hierarchy of needs theory, Herzberg's two factor theory, ERG theory, equity theory, and expectancy theory.

Geographical Scope: Due to cost, time frame and research capacity, 7Up Bottling Company PLC, Aba, Abia State will be the area of study, which is expected to take at most one year to complete.

Level of Analysis: In this study, the organizational level analysis is the unit of analysis. Organizational performance is the dependent variable while planning and control, which entail contingency planning, tactical planning, operational control and human and machine control are the independent variables. Employees at all levels in the company will be understudied.

1.7   Significance of the Study

Without mincing words, different researches have in the past considered planning and control and its influence on different organizations, particularly as it relates to employees' performance, which determines performance in such establishments. What has not been fully established however, is the outright positive effects of such researches on the productive nature of most organizations in Nigeria, particularly those in the South-South and South-Eastern parts of the country.

This study will enlighten managers on the importance of proper planning and control in enhancing organizational performance. The study will also ensure the need for employers to create enabling environments to encourage employees' participation in the overall growth of the organization. The result of this research work will also contribute to the advancement of the existing body of knowledge on planning and control as well as organizational performance. It will also be of great importance to professionals in the management sector and researchers, including students, who would find the work very useful for their studies and research works.

1.8   Organization of the Project Report

This study, like other academic research in the faculty, will be organized into five distinct chapters as follows;

- Chapter one focuses on the background of the study, statement of the research problem, research questions, research objectives, research hypotheses, scope of the study, significance of the study and organization of the study.

- Chapter two is the literature review. It covers the literature reviews and theoretical framework of the study. To be reviewed are works and opinions of authors with respect to the impact of planning and control on organizational performance.

- Chapter three contains the methodology of the study. It is the blue print of the project.

- Chapter four dwells into the data presentation and analysis gathered in the course of study and

- Chapter five is the last chapter that summarizes, recommends and concludes the study.

CHAPTER TWO

LITERATURE REVIEW

2.1   Conceptual Clarifications

2.1.1   Introduction

Planning and controlling as a pertinent tool for ensuring organization performance is very necessary. Therefore, a constant and comprehensive step in formulating strategic plans and putting in place certain appraisals and evaluating the system as a measure to control become necessary. The absence of planning and control limits productive rate and growth of an organization.

In majority of organizations in Nigeria, planning is the most important management tool for performance and performance and for organizations to perform well, resources must be well utilized and customers well served. To achieve such ends, all of an organization's human and material resources must be well utilized in the right way and the right time to create high quality products at minimal cost.

Performance is a summary measure of the quantity and quality of work performance, with resources utilization taken into account. It can be measured at the individual, group, or organizations level. Performance may be expressed as success into dimensions of organizations performance, effectiveness and efficiency, which serve as the means by which goods and services are provided beyond the boundaries of an individual or small group's capacity of self-sufficiency. Such provision, also acknowledged, may be made for profit through some other more controlled framework of commercial or social provision (Dawson 2013).

However, Planning on the other hand, is regarded as the most basic of all the management functions. It involves the selecting from among alternative future course of action for the organization as a whole and every department or section within it. Furthermore, it requires selecting organizational objectives and departmental goals, determines and provides a rational approach to pre-selected objectives. It strongly implies managerial innovation and the ability to create something (Koontz 2000). The problem which underscores the need to undertake this study is aptly described by Koontz et al (2000) with all the interest in planning and all the sense of urgency brought about by modern super competition, is the danger that planning can become merely a costly fad, not very useful and even disillusioning.

The implication of the above assertion is that not all organizations that plan eventually reap the desired benefits. Schermerhorn (2009) adds that most planning failures arise from their inability of managers to truly understand the planning and to implement it well. Problems have been identified in the planning process. For instance, in setting objectives, organizations find it difficult to involve employees, shareholders, customers etc. closely related to this is the issue associated with the likely environment different variables and events. However, the objective of the study is to determine the relationship between effective planning and control and organizational Performance and to also examine whether effective Planning brings employees Performance in an organization.

2.1.2   Planning

Planning is an ever-future present modern life. Although there is no universal approach, virtually everyone is a planner, at least in the information sense. A plan therefore, is a specific documented intention, consisting of an objective, which does not stop abruptly. It is an ongoing process that reflects and adapts to changes in the environment and it is a fundamental and primary management function.

Koontz and O'Donnel (2000) define planning as a deciding in advance on what to do, how to do it, when to do it and who is to do it. Planning bridges the gap between where one is now and where one would like to be in the future; it makes it possible for things to happen. Through planning, the manager is able to anticipate the possible effects of forces, which will change the objective of the business. Planning is particularly very important in developing nations, where resources are relatively scarce. Planning is the blueprint for action.

An important aspect of the managerial revolution of the past four decades has been said to be the tremendous interest in planning by all forms of enterprises such as business, government, educational institutions and others. The importance of planning in areas such as factory operations has been stressed many years earlier. For instance, production managers discovered early that without planning, their mistakes showed up within days, as production line came to a halt because of a misfit part or the absence of a needed component.

Goetz 2000 opined that Planning is fundamentally choosing and planning problems arise only when an alternative course of action is discovered. As such, Goetz saw planning as being inextricable linked with decision-making. But Koontz et al (2000) conceives planning to be much more than essentially decision-making. According to them, planning presupposed the existence of alternatives, and that there are very few decisions for which some kind of alternative does not exist. They state further that planning is deciding in advance what to do, how to do it, when to do it, and who is to do it.

As the most basic of all managerial functions, planning involves selecting from among alternatives, future courses of action for the enterprise as a whole and for every depart mental goals and determining ways of achieving them. The authors argue that planning must involve an open-system approach to managing. This is because planning cannot be taken in a vacuum. Rather, it must consider the nature of the future environment in which planning decisions and actions are intended to operate. Stoner (2005) offers that planning is a process that does not end when a plan is agreed upon; rather, it must be implemented. Also at any time during the implantation and control process, plans may require modification to avoid becoming useless or even damaging. Stoner's argument therefore, implies that decisions must be made at many points in the planning process. For instance, managers must decide which predictions in such areas as the economy, and the actions of competitions are likely to be most accurate. They must also analyze organizational resources and decide how to allocate them to achieve their goals most effectively.

2.1.2.1 Aspects of Planning

Koontz et al (2000) mentioned an issue known as the nature of planning which can be highlighted as four aspects of planning. These aspects are contributions to purpose and objectives, primary of planning, pervasiveness of planning and efficiency of plans.

Contribution to purpose and objectives- Drawing mainly from the work of Goetz, Koontz and his colleagues assert that the purpose of every plan and all derivative plans is to facilitate the accomplishment of enterprise purpose and objectives. This principle derives from the nature of organized enterprise, which exists for the accomplishment of group purpose, through deliberate cooperative efforts by all members of the organization.

Primary of planning- It is argued that since managerial operations entail organizing, staffing, creating and controlling, which are designed to support the accomplishment of enterprise objectives, then planning should logically precede the execution of all other managerial functions. Although all the managerial functions are interlinked in practice as a system of action, planning is unique, in that it establishes the objective necessary for all group effort. Besides, it is argued that plans must be made to accomplish these objectives before the manager knows what kind of organization relationships and personal qualifications are needed, along which course subordinates are to be directed and led, what control is to be applied. Most important, all the other managerial functions must be planned if they are to be effective Koontz et al (2000).

Pervasiveness of planning- This implies that planning is a function of all managers, although the character and breadth of planning will vary with the nature of policies and plans authorized by their superiors. However, one manager because of his authority or position in the organization may do more planning or more important planning or another, or the planning of one may be more basic and applicable to a large portion of enterprises than that of another Koontz et al (2000).

Efficiency of plans- According to Koontz et al (2000), this concept stresses that a plan is efficient when it contributes to purpose and objectives as offset by the cost and other unsought consequences required to formulate and operate such plans. As such a plan too high attracts unnecessarily high costs. Also, even though the concepts of efficiency implies the normal ratio of input to output in terms of money, labor hours or units of production to include such values as individual and group satisfaction. In all, it can be concluded that if managers do not plan to some degree, they would have no idea of whether or not the organization is accomplishing its purpose.

Dixon (2011) provides four reasons why planning is important for good management. They are as follows:

1) Planning aids the process of control, because mangers have a benchmark against which they can measure the actual results achieved.

2) Planning helps to make the operations of organization more economical.

3) Planning focuses attention on the organization's real objectives.

4) Planning helps to offset the effects of uncertainty and change.

He however, warns that this does not imply that planning remove, or even transcend the presence of risk, but it does make managers more aware of the risk involved. However, Plans emerge or are formulated during the planning process. These plans also differ. In fact it has been argued that failure of some managers to recognize the variety of plans has often caused difficulty in making planning effective.

2.1.2.2 Important Parts of Planning

He further explains that planning horizon is an important part of any plan. In the planning horizon, the length of time specifies for activities to be carried out. Three planning horizon can be identified: long range, intermediate and short range.

1. **Long-range planning-** Involves identifying those activities to be performed over an extended period of time. Long range plan may extend for several decades. It is different from strategic planning, which is primarily concerned with how the organization will position itself among competing firms in a market. Long-range planning identifies the activities to be performed that will lead to the accomplishment of official goals. One important feature is that a long-range plan is necessarily different from shorter planning horizons in a plan covering 20 years.

2. **Intermediate Planning-** Identifies activities to be carried out over a period of five years at the middle levels of the organization. Intermediate planning is critical in most cases to the success. It focuses more on the activities that have to be carried out with a planning horizon that contains fewer uncertainties.

3. **Short-range Planning:** Developing plans for implementation within a planning horizon of less than one year is often referred to as short-range planning. Short-range plans may specify activities to be carried out that will achieve certain production levels each week. While short-range plans are necessary for most organizations, they can have drawbacks. Often, managers become so focused on short-range plans. Ultimately, this can lead to failure in the accomplishment of organizational goals. There are several steps in planning process used by large, diversified corporation.

   Statement of official goals: The chief executive of the firm sets the official goals usually presenting them to division heads. A formal statement of the official goals provides a common focus for planning and identifies those goals that top management seek to emphasize.

Development of the Divisional plans: Divisional mangers receive copies of the official goals and begin divisional plans. Operative goals are identified to support the official goals.

Consolidation of the Divisional and departmental plans: Each division submits its plans to top management, which then consolidates the divisional objectives into consistent package across divisions. In this step, top management may either reject plans, accept plans in the plans submitted by the divisions.

Co-ordination of the Divisional plans: After preparation of the divisional plans has been completed, the plans are returned to top management. Top management aggregates the divisional plans, checks computation and evaluates the plans based on financial criteria.

Integration of divisional Budgets: The completion of divisional budgets leads to the final step where the budgets are submitted to top management. Top management reviews the budgets but rarely rejects them. This is because it is often felt that top management does not have detailed knowledge of operations at the lower levels of the cooperation to make a critical examination of those plans. According to Schermerhom (2010) the process of management involves planning, organizing, leading, and controlling. The first of these functions, planning, set the stage for the others. It is a process of deciding exactly what one wants to accomplish and how to go about it. When planning is done well, it creates a solid platform for further management efforts at organizing, allocating, and arranging resources to accomplish essential tasks.

The planning process identifies the specific result or desired outcome of the plan as a statement of action and steps to be taken in order to accomplish the objectives.

Step 1: Define your objective, identify desired outcome or results in any specific ways, know where you want to go, be specific enough that you will know you have arrived when you get there or know how far off the mark you are at various points along the way.

Step 2: Determine where you start vis-à-vis objectives. Evaluate current accomplishments to the desired results, know what strengths work in your favour and the weakness that may hold you back.

Step 3: Develop premises regarding future conditions. Try to anticipate future events, generate alternative "scenarios" for what may happen for each scenario, things that may help towards your objectives.

Step 4: Analyze possible action alternatives, choose the best among them and decide how to implement. List and carefully evaluate the possible actions that may be taken, choosing the alternative most likely to accomplish your objectives.

Step 5: Implement the plan and evaluate results. Take action and carefully measure your progress toward objectives. Do what the plan as needed.

He further explains that a strategic plan is comprehensive and addresses long-term needs and directions of the organization while an operational plan is of limited scope and addresses activities to implement strategic plans and achieve strategic objectives. While plan tools and techniques are clearly essential to the success of the management process, the benefits, however, are most often realized when the planning approaches are comprehensive and the foundations are well established. In the latter regards, the useful planning tools and techniques include forecasting, the use of scenarios, benchmarking, participative planning and the use of staff planners. Forecasting is the process of making assumptions about what will happen in the future. All good plans involve forecasts. In the final analysis, forecasting always relies on human judgment.

2.1.2.3 Types of Planning

1. **Tactical Planning:** Tactical planning involves determining the steps a business must take to reach the objectives developed through strategic planning. Tactical plans will inevitably change as your strategic goals and aspects of the business context change. These plans have a relatively short time frame, shorter than the time frame of your

strategic plans, as Ricky W. Griffin says in "Fundamentals of Management" (2005. While your broader goals may remain the same, how you accomplish them and which step of the process you are in will change. This calls for a new tactical plan. You will need different tactical plans to achieve your business' goals and objectives. Objectives such as becoming the leader in your niche market, using responsible business practices, cultivating an experienced team and taking your business to foreign markets each require a separate tactical plan.

2. **Contingency Planning:** Contingency planning involves planning what a business will do if something goes wrong, such as a failure of the original business plan, a lawsuit or an emergency situation caused by a natural disaster, as Williams (2002) says in "The Worst That Could Happen," on Entrepreneur. Contingency plans may change little, particularly when they plan for unlikely situations such as a tornado. Your contingency plans may remain unchanged for years, except for adaptations to the scale of your business and company changes.

2.1.2.4 How Management Planning Affects the Achievement of Goals and Objectives

For an organization to be effective and efficient, it must have a clear mission. Such mission should periodically be defined as an era of rigid change. The mission of an organization must be clearly published as it is the correct one of any organization system that will effectively guide it through a certain period of time. Such mission should provide a focal point for the entire planning process, Parkinson, 2014).

According to Nnenna Ani, 2002, contributions to purpose are part of the essentials of planning. The purpose of every plan is to facilitate the accomplishment of enterprise, purpose and objectives. Plan alone cannot make an enterprise successful, action is required. Plans can however, focus on action and purpose. They can forecast which actions will lead towards the ultimate objectives or which one is irrelevant. Management planning seeks to achieve a consistent coordinated structure of operation, focused on desired ends. Without plans, actions must become merely random, actively producing nothing, but chaos.

According to Agbo (2000), all managerial operations are designed to support the accomplishment of enterprise objectives. Planning logically proceed the execution of all other management functions inter-mesh in practice. Planning is unique in that, it establishes the objective necessary for all groups' efforts. Planning precedes all other managerial functions. As in the above diagram, plans must be made to accomplish organizational objectives before managers know the kinds of qualifications are needed. Also, what course subordinates, are to be directed to lead and what kind of control is to be applied. Also, all other managerial functions are inseparable, unplanned action cannot be controlled because one would not know when there are deviations from expected course of action.

2.1.2.5 How Efficient Planning Affects the Profit of an Organization

Inefficient planning is being measured by the loss, which an organization encounters if their resources are not properly utilized. According to Stoner (2002), planning must follow the principles. Any plan that does not follow the principles of planning may be regarded as inefficient planning because it may affect the profit of any organization at the long-run, thereby yielding low profit or loss.

Obi (2005) explains the following principles;

i. **Clearly defined objectives:** Planning as we know is the selection of course of action, the action should aim an objective of goal which is an end result of the action, if the plan does not help to achieve, it is a failure. A good plan is a path to objective achievement.

ii. **Simple to understand:** Complexity of plans leads to confusion and impossibility of accomplishment. Plans must therefore be simple to understand and not ambiguous.

iii. **Consistency:** Plans are not meant to be contradictory. They should be sequential where possible.

iv. **Flexibility:** Plans are expected to be accommodating and prone to be adaptive and not rigid. Plans must be such as to make provisions for expansion.

v. **Adequate information:** one of the greatest ingredients for planning is adequate and complete information. A good plan that is expected to expand profit must be based on the information collected and such information must be stated in the plan for future review.

vi. **Standard and balance:** Plans are expected to be of a standard quality and to be balanced. Under standard plans lead to poor quality outputs. When there is standard plan, it will be easy to effect control. Standard plan must have undergone test before it can be regarded as that.

vii. **Practicability and feasibility:** Plans should be practicable when they are made, and when they cannot be practicable, they become wasteful and useless.

viii. **Economy:** Plans are not expected to be very expensive. Therefore, planners must consider the resources available while planning, in order to avoid loss.

Nwachukwu (2011), in his book identified six steps in the planning process. The processes are diagrammatically presented below:

2.1.2.6 Problems of Planning

i. **Lack Of Basic Demographic Statistics:** Inadequate or absence of statistical records showing the actual population figures of some communities, age, sex, distribution of the population, etc. constituted a stumbling block to planning in this part of the world. (Nnenna 2002).

ii. **Absence of basic planning statistics:** The complete absence of educationally, qualified and honest personnel basic equipment with which planning processes would be facilitated stand in the forefront against effective planning.

iii. **Lack of continuity of top management position:** The incessant changes of the top management executive, especially in government parastatals inhibit the proper implementation of good policy measures. In fact, the instability in management and board of these parastatals has a side effect. Every new administration begins by dissolving the boards of all parastatals and government owned companies and appointing new members to replace them. This process do not give room for good planning programmes (Ojemba, 2000).

iv. **Rapid but devastating change in government policies:** For example, the ban of some organizations in the cold and in the dark planning like any other management function is not always easy and as such, number of factors impede effective planning.

v. **Rapid changes in the environment:** Business today is done in a dynamic environment and not in a static one. Businesses are subjected to some changes. The degrees of instability are complexity caused by some social dynamics, varying considerably from industry. The instability of the business environment and rapid changes make it to be very successful and problematic.

vi. **Delegation of planning responsibility:** Top management assures that it can delegate its planning responsibility and thus not become directly involved in management planning.

vii. **Insufficient planning time:** Weihrick (2003) opines that management becomes too involve in current problems that devoted insufficient time to planning. As a result, planning becomes discredited at lower level. Many times, managers are to carry out contingent plans. Such should use much skill, but little time is given them.

Steiner (2002) includes management failure, clearly defined and developed goals that are suitable basis for formulating long range plans. Some managers are reluctant to set goals for many reasons: Lack of information, fear of the future, government control and regulation, poor rewards system and so on. These become impediments to planning.

2.1.3 Controlling

Controlling is one of the key functions of management. Planning and control go hand-in-hand for without efficient planning and control, the organization cannot achieve any objective. It can also be seen as a primary goal-oriented function of management in an organization. It is a process of comparing the actual performance with the set standards of the company to ensure that activities are performed according to the plans and if not, then take corrective actions. Controlling starts as soon as the execution phase starts in order to determine if plans are being realized. Controlling is that phase of the management process which maintains organization activity within allowable limit as measures from expectations. These expectations may be implicit or explicitly stated in terms of objectives, plans, procedures or rules and regulations. Controlling can be seen as part of management activities undertaken to ensure that outcomes are consistent with planned organizational activities.

Control requires the establishment of standards, information process and taking of corrective actions. In controlling, management is not only concerned with measuring performance and Performance against standard, but also evaluating the performance to see if there are deviations or exceptions from the original plan. The reasons for the deviation are sought so that appropriate corrective actions could be taken.

2.1.3.1 Features of Controlling

An effective control system has the following features:

- It helps in achieving organizational goals.

- Facilitates optimum utilization of resources.

- It evaluates the accuracy of the standard.

- It also sets discipline and order.

- Motivates the employees and boosts employee morale.

- Ensures future planning by revising standards.

- Improves overall performance of an organization.

- It also minimizes errors.

2.1.3.2 Advantages of Control

The advantages of control to management cannot be overstated, as planning without control is useless since there is no other effective means of determining if the plan objective is being realized. Some of the major advantages of control to the organization are stated below.

1. Control guides behaviour toward useful organizational ends: Lack of control results in erratic behaviour that may be only tangent to organizational goals.

2. Control ensures that resources are effectively utilized: It helps to avoid the waste of useful resources in useless endeavours or inefficient operations.

3. Control focuses attention on factors essential in achieving organizational effectiveness: It helps to focus attention in meeting performance criteria, quality standards, and achieving goals.

4. Control encourages the action necessary to maintain performance for Performance.

2.1.3.3 Types of Control

Operational Control

The concept of organizational control is implicit in the bureaucratic theory of Max Weber. Associated with this theory are such concepts as "span of control", "closeness of supervision", and "hierarchical authority". Weber's view tends to include all levels or types of organizational control as being the same. More recently, writers have tended to differentiate the control process between that which emphasizes the nature of the organizational or systems design and that which deals with daily operations. To illustrate the difference, we "evaluate" the performance of a system to see how effective and efficient the design proved to be or to discover why it failed. In contrast, we operate and "control" the system with respect to the daily inputs of material, information, and energy. In both instances, the elements of feedback are present, but organizational control tends to review and evaluate the nature and arrangement of components in the system, whereas operational control tends to adjust the daily inputs, (Nnenna 2002).

The direction for organizational control comes from the goals and strategic plans of the organization. General plans are translated into specific performance measures such as share of the market, earnings, return on investment, and budgets. The process of organizational control is to review and evaluate the performance of the system against these established norms. Rewards for meeting or exceeding standards may range from special recognition to salary increases or promotions. On the other hand, a failure to meet expectations may signal the need to reorganize or redesign (Nnenna, 2002).

When a system has failed or is in great difficulty, special diagnostic techniques may be required to isolate the trouble areas and to identify the causes of the difficulty. It is appropriate to investigate areas that have been troublesome before or areas where some measure of performance can be quickly identified. For example, if an organization's output backlog builds rapidly, it is logical to check first to see if the problem is due to such readily obtainable measures as increased demand or to a drop in available man hours. When a more detailed analysis is necessary, a systematic procedure should be followed (Nnenna, 2002)

Human and Machine Control

The elements of control are easy to identify in machine systems. For example, the characteristic to be controlled might be some variable like speed or temperature, and the sensing device could be a speedometer or a thermometer. An expectation of precision exists because the characteristic is quantifiable and the standard and the normal variation to be expected can be described in exact terms. In automatic machine systems, inputs of information are used in a process of continual adjustment to achieve output specifications. When even a small variation from the standard occurs, the correction process begins. The automatic system is highly structured, designed to accept certain kinds of input and produce specific output, and programmed to regulate the transformation of inputs within a narrow range of variation (Nnenna, 2002).

In human control systems, the relationship between objectives and associated characteristics is often vague; the measurement of the characteristic may be extremely subjective; the expected standard is difficult to define; and the amount of new inputs required is impossible to quantify. To illustrate, let us refer once more to a formalized social system in which deviant behaviour is controlled through a process of observed violation of the existing law (sensing), court hearings and trials (comparison with standard), incarceration when the accused is found guilty (correction), and release from custody after rehabilitation of the individual has occurred.

Most organized systems are some combination of man and machine; some elements of control may be performed by machine whereas others are accomplished by man. In addition, some standards may be precisely structured whereas others may be little more than general guidelines with wide variations expected in output. Man must act as the controller when measurement is subjective and judgment is required. Machines such as computers are incapable of making exceptions from the specified control criteria regardless of how much a particular case might warrant special consideration. A pilot acts in conjunction with computers and automatic pilots to fly large jets. In the event of unexpected weather changes, or possible collision with another plane, he must intercede and assume direct control (Nnenna, 2002)

2.1.3.4 Steps of Control

Establishing standards: This means setting up of the target which needs to be achieved to meet organizational goals eventually. Standards indicate the criteria of performance. Control standards are categorized as quantitative and qualitative standards. Quantitative standards are expressed in terms of money while Qualitative standards, on the other hand, include intangible items.

Measurement of actual performance: The actual performance of the employee is measured against the target. With the increasing levels of management, the measurement of performance becomes difficult.

Comparison of actual performance with the standard: This compares the degree of difference between the actual performance and the standard.

Taking corrective actions: It is initiated by the manager who corrects any defects in actual performance.

Controlling process thus regulates companies' activities so that actual performance conforms to the standard plan. An effective control system enables managers to avoid circumstances which cause the company's loss. Controlling and planning are interrelated for controlling gives an important input into the next planning cycle. Controlling is a backwards-looking function which brings the management cycle back to the planning function. Planning is a forward-looking process as it deals with the forecasts about the future conditions, Stoner et al (2002).

2.1.4   Organizational Performance

In a formal sense, Performance refers to how well an organization converts input (such as labour, materials, machines and capital) into goods and services or output. But today it is no longer limited to measuring ratios of inputs and outputs. Basically, increasing Performance just means working smarter.

One of the most important issues facing the applied behavioural sciences is that of human Performance, the quality and quantity of work. Performance concerns both effectiveness and efficiency. According to Drucker (2002), a founding father of management theory, effectiveness is a minimum condition for survival after success has been achieved. Efficiency is concerned with doing things right and effectiveness is doing the right things.

Stoner (2002) suggested a clear example of a person placing personal goals before organizational goals, in bureaucracies, managers often try to build up their own departments by adding unnecessary personnel and more equipment. Although, this tendency may increase the prestige and importance of the managers. This, in discussing effectiveness, we must recognize the differences between individual goals, organizational goals, leadership and management. So their successes measured by the output or Performance of the group they lead, with that thought in mind, Bernard Bass (2015) suggested a clear distinction between successful and effective leadership and management. Success has to do with how the individual or the group behaves; on the other hand effectiveness describes the internal state of an individual and thus, it is attitudinal in nature. Individuals who are interested only in success tend to emphasize their position power and use close supervision.

Effective individuals however, will also depend on personal power and use more general supervision. Position power tends to be delegated down through the organization, while personal power is generated upward from below through follower acceptance.

Luthans (2017) conducted a four-year observational study to determine similarities and differences noted that successful managers spent more of their time and effort networking with others inside and outside the organization than did effective managers. In the management of organizations, the difference between successful and effective often explain why many supervisors can get a satisfactory level of output only when they are right there looking over a worker's shoulder. Managers could be successful but ineffective having only a short-lived influence over the behaviour of others. It should be pointed out that this successful versus effective framework is a way of evaluating the response to a specific behavioural event and not of evaluating performance over time. And so what comes in mind is what determines organizational effectiveness.

2.1.5   Influence of Planning and Controlling on Organizational Performance

According to Munive-Hernandez, Dewhurst, Pritchard and Barber (2004), planning and controlling involve the plan or pattern of act that adds company main goals, policies and action systems unified into a whole. Aldehayyat and Khattab (2011) noted that planning and controlling methods empower managers to convert data into valued decisions and appropriate actions. Sorel and Pennequin (2008) advocates for planning and controlling to involve developing objectives or the organizational strategic plans and looking for resources that would best be suited in achieving the organizational goals as outlined in strategic plans. Each goal should have financial and human resource projections associated with its completion so that it becomes successful. The planning and controlling process also creates timelines for when the plans should be achieved. According to Ballou (2007), planning also involves developing the tracking and assessment method that will be used to monitor the project process.

Planning is normally where the direction of the business is made through a multiplicity of activities comprising the making of goals and controlling. As such, the planning function of management symbolizes numerous points of decision making (Schraeder, 2015). Daft and Marcic (2016) also identified the third effect of planning and controlling on organizational Performance as its pervasiveness. The entire managers starting from the every superintendent to the utmost officer who is the Chief Executive Officer (CEO) of a business are supposed to engage in planning and controlling.

At the lower levels, it may be termed as operational planning while at the highest levels it is termed as strategic planning. The time spent in planning in any level depends on the level type. The CEOs may be involved more in engaging in activities such as organizing and planning, whilst head of departments are more involved in areas leading people, acquiring resources in the respective departments and the control of performance and Performance in the departments. The more efficient the plans are the more they contribute to improved organizational Performance.

According to Awino (2012) positive change is caused by effective planning. The efficiency of plans must be aligned to add to the aims of the business and to promote the analyzing and improvement of strategies. Koontz and O'Donnell (2011) particularly viewed that efficiency feature has to be used not only in monetary terms to numerous resources used in service and production actions, but also to the group and individual gratification of human resources.

Sosiawani, et al., (2015) state that each dimension of strategic planning all contribute to organizational performance. Formality of strategic planning and control has been identified to have positive relationship with organizational performance (Glaister, et al., 2008). The tools of strategic planning are believed to be capable to increase the effectiveness and efficiency of business planning (Kraus, Harms & Schwarz, 2006). These tools include the SWOT analysis, interrelationship diagram and affinity diagrams. By using tools of strategic planning, business would be capable to attain improved performance and Performance (Aldehayyat & Khattab, 2013). There is also positive relationship between employee participation and firms' performance. It is believed that employee's participation effect on strategic planning contributes to the effectiveness and the development of strategy which in turn, leads to better effectiveness in the implementation.

Employees contribute in planning by giving their suggestion and test-driving the different strategies so as to get the best fit in terms of strategies that an organization can adopt, resulting in increased performance (Collier, Fishwick & Floyd, 2004). Whenever employees participate in crafting the plan development of a business, their motivation and attachment to the project is high, thus making them more effective while running the project. Veettil (2008) showed that by applying strategic planning correctly, would be able to contribute to companies achieving better performance. Consequently, creating assignments with timelines, considering the ability of individual employees in the completion of the task time horizon is also considered as the key element of strategic planning which is capable to advance the performance of the business.

Mitchelmore and Rowley (2013) through their study, assert that businesses need to lengthen their time horizon of strategic planning for them to achieve better performance and Performance. Since enough time allocated will allow employees to work efficiently without the pressure that time is running out on them, this means that their performance would be greatly improved. There are various implementation strategies that management in different organizations can adopt. The strategies may adopt a top-down approach where the policies and plans are developed at the top and the information trickles down to the bottom where the instructions are carried out. The implementation approach may also be bottom-up or hybrid depending on the organization structure and their internal systems of handling firm's assignments (Veettil, 2008).

Another element of strategic planning is the control of planning (Kraus, 2006). Wagaki (2013) describes strategic planning and controlling as a continuing, never-ending, combined process demanding unceasing review and improvement. Strategic planning is thus considered and developing, vigorous and a collaborating process. To build your company to a performing and productive level within the industry, the business has to strategize and employ the use of strategic planning practices. These are key characteristics which are vital towards founding and positioning the business strategically in the market (Kathama, 2012). Aldehayyat and Twaissi (2011) have shown in their study that the relationship midst strategic planning and companies' performance is a significant and positive relationship.

2.1.6 Conceptual Framework

The diagram below shows the relationship between the four variables explained above and how they influence organizational Performance.

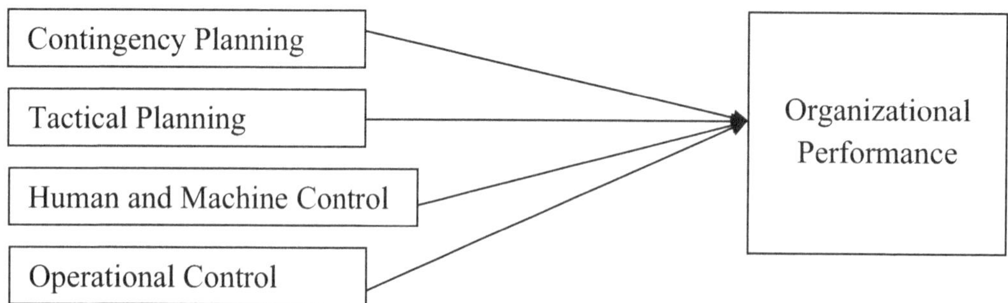

Source: Researcher Model (2020).

2.1.6.1 Contingency Planning as a Measure for Enhancing Organizational Performance

For most businesspeople, the term contingency planning conjures images of natural disasters, such as hurricanes, tornadoes, earthquakes or flood and manmade crises like riots, fires or terrorism. The concept of contingency planning is really tied in with routine business performance management. That is because many companies fail to recognize how important it is to describe in advance, in detail, the steps the organization will take in events that it fails to meet or conversely, in the event that it exceeds its budget and performance as well as Performance plans. For any organization to be productive, managers or planners should have a number of different contingency plans to address emergency situations that could arise, as each may require a different course of action. Consider the types of natural disasters that could occur in the business environment. Each must have its own plan, so as to most effectively ensure the safety of the employees, customers and business. The organization should also consider what other types of risk the business faces, such as a lawsuit from an employee. In nutshell, in enhancing organizational Performance, there must be a proper contingency plan (Obinna, 2016).

2.1.6.2 Tactical Planning as a Measure for Enhancing Organizational Performance

The role of tactical plans is an activity that is said to be inherent in everything a manager does. In reality, the essence of every organization is for the organization to achieve its goals effectively and efficiently. It follows therefore that such goals and objectives cannot be achieved just like that; it needs all the required planning inputs to attain the targeted goals of the organization.

Tactical plans are meant to increase probability that the organization will achieve its objectives. This follows therefore that steps in tactical plans should not be violated. If these steps are not strictly adhered to in tactical plans, there is likelihood that the objectives of the organization will not be achieved.

2.1.6.3 Human and Machine Control as a Measure for Enhancing Organizational Performance

Continued development of modern machines and production equipment, supported by advanced control systems and based on recent achievements in computer and software technology, it is necessary to fulfill client requirements. A significant number of manufacturing systems are able to work automatically with a limited contribution from employees. However, even in advanced manufacturing systems, one of the most important factors is still the human being (Obinna, 2016).

Usually overall system performance depends on human decisions, and the significance of such decisions is higher than it was in the past because of more complex and costly production systems. In such a situation, the efficient utilization of manufacturing equipment via proper man-machine interaction is necessary.

It would not be out of place to state that Human and Machine control, being one of the most important components which gear toward organizational Performance, should often be considered from the start-up of the organizational. When machines are properly regulated and humans effectively managed to achieve business objectives, such performance would enhance the Performance measure of the organization (Obinna, 2016).

2.1.6.4 Operational Control as a Measure for Enhancing Organizational Performance

In contrast to organizational control, operational control serves to regulate the day-to-day output relative to schedules, specifications, and costs. Is the output of product or service the proper quality and is it available as scheduled? Are inventories of raw materials, goods-in-process, and finished products being purchased and produced in the desired quantities? Are the costs associated with the transformation process in line with cost estimates? Is the information needed in the transformation process available in the right form and at the right time? Is the energy resource being utilized efficiently?

The most difficult task of management concerns monitoring the behavior of individuals, comparing performance to some standard and providing rewards or punishment as indicated (Obinna, 2016).

Sometimes this control over people relates entirely to their output. For example, a manager might not be concerned with the behavior of a salesman as long as sales were as high as expected. In other instances, close supervision of the salesman might be appropriate if achieving customer satisfaction were one of the sales organization's main objectives.

The larger the unit, the more likely that the control characteristic will be related to some output goal. It also follows that if it is difficult or impossible to identify the actual output of individuals, it is better to measure the performance of the entire group. This means that individuals' levels of motivation and the measurement of their performance become subjective judgments made by the supervisor. Controlling output also suggests the difficulty of controlling individuals' performance and relating this to the total system's objectives (Obinna, 2016).

2.2 Review of Related Theories

2.2.1 Content Theories of Work Motivation

The main interest of content theories is to find out what controls and organizes the human behavior. They are mainly concerned with what motivates people, and what kind of rewards can enhance people's satisfaction and performance. According to Analoui (2000), the content theories have identified needs, incentives and the work itself as important factors that contribute towards job satisfaction and focus on the inner drivers of human behavior. Accordingly, they can be described as "static" theories because "they incorporate only one or a few points in time and are either past-or present-time oriented." Hence, they are not very useful in predicting people's behavior, but they can be used in understanding the factors that motivate people in their working environment.

Although there are a number of content theories in the field of work motivation, we will mainly concentrate on three of the most prominent and known content theories of work motivation. These theories are Maslow's Need Hierarchy, Herzeberg's Two Factor Theory, and Alderfer's ERG Theory.

2.2.1.1 Maslow's Hierarchy of Needs Theory

The Hierarchy of Needs Theory is considered one of the most famous theories in the field of human motivation and one of the first theories that attempt to describe the human behavior toward satisfying the different human needs (Kreitner, 2009). The theory is based on the assumption that a need affects a person's activities until he or she satisfies it (Steers, 2010), thus the main motivator of people is their desire to satisfy their needs. Maslow thought that personal needs can be arranged in a hierarchical order; in essence, once one of these needs has been satisfied, it will temporally lose its effect as a motivator and the person will focus on satisfying the next higher need which has been activated (Hilgert and Leonard, 2007; Luthans, 2000).

Steers (2010) demonstrated that, according to the Hierarchy Theory, people move from the bottom to the top of the need hierarchy through an active cycle of deprivation, domination, gratification and activation. As, when a person feels deprivation (unsatisfied need) in one of the hierarchy levels, this will direct his action toward satisfying this particular need. For example, if the person needs to satisfy his safety and security needs, he will temporarily ignore satisfying his higher-order needs; however, once he has met this need, the higher need will be activated and he will try to satisfy it, thus repeating this cycle of action until he reaches the apex of the need hierarchy.

2.2.1.2 Herzberg's Two Factor Theory

In 1959, Herzberg and his colleagues introduced the "Two Factor Theory" which is one of the most well-known theories in the management field. His study was conducted based on semi-structured interviews of a sample of 203 accountants and engineers from a business enterprise in Pittsburgh. The aim of the study was to identify the moments when the participant felt good or bad about his or her job. Participants were asked two questions; the first was to describe in detail the times that they felt good about their job, and the second was to describe in detail the times when they felt bad about their job (Herzberg, 1959).

On the basis of the answers of these questions, Herzberg classified the job factors into two main categories. He called the first "hygiene" and the second "motivators". He argued that hygiene factors resulted largely from extrinsic factors (e.g. company policy, interpersonal relations, working conditions, pay, status, and job security) and were mainly found in employees' descriptions of the bad events (negative events). These factors are related with work environment and can hardly provide a real feeling of job satisfaction. However, when these factors fall below the acceptable level for the employee, job dissatisfaction emerges as a result. He also argued that all a person can expect when satisfying the hygiene factors is to prevent the feeling of dissatisfaction and the poor levels of job performance, as its existence will help remove the barriers to achieve job satisfaction. Therefore, the hygiene factors offer little chance for self actualization because they do not offer the employees the chances for responsibility or achievement (Carrel, 2000).

On the other hand, "motivators" (e.g. achievement, recognition, work itself, responsibility, advancement, and possibility of growth) were related to the content and nature of the job itself (Steers, 2010) and were mainly found in employees' descriptions of the good events (positive events). These motivators offer a better chance for self-actualization and creativity. Accordingly, the only way for employees to achieve satisfaction and motivation is by using the motivators. However, the absence of these factors will not lead to job dissatisfaction, as in the case of the absence of the hygiene factors, but the result will reach the "neutral state" as in the case of the existence of the hygiene factors (Herzberg *et al.*, 1959). Consequently, to reach job satisfaction there are two stages that must be fulfilled. The first is to eliminate job dissatisfaction by satisfying the employee's hygiene factors, this will just bring the employee's satisfaction to zero point (neutral state). The motivators can then be used to remove the employee's satisfaction from zero point to a positive level of job satisfaction (Herzberg, 1959).

Herzberg's ideas were different from other researchers in that other researchers dealt with satisfaction and dissatisfaction as opposites, while Herzberg thought that satisfaction and the factors that lead to satisfaction are totally different to those factors that lead to job dissatisfaction; he believed that the opposite of satisfaction is zero satisfaction, while the opposite of dissatisfaction is zero dissatisfaction (Herzberg, 1959).

The Two-Factor Theory is a superior theory that has made a great contribution to managerial knowledge as it clarifies the different sources of job attitudes. It had an explanatory power that inspired researchers and generated a huge volume of refreshes in the field of industrial psychology (Whitsett and Winslow, 2011). One of the greatest contributions of Herzberg's theory was to shed light on the content of work motivation, emphasizing that management are not motivating their employees when focusing only on the hygiene factors, and that only a challenging job that includes the possibility for achievement, advancement, responsibility, recognition, and growth can motivate people (Luthans, 2000). Moreover, Herzberg"s theory has received some support from researchers, as many studies show a general support of Herzberg's idea that factors leading to job satisfaction (motivators) are different from, and not simply opposite to, factors leading to job dissatisfaction (hygienes). This idea was supported by the investigations of several researchers (Halpern, 1962; Centers & Bugental, 1966; Saleh and Grygior, 1969; Soliman, 1970; Myers, 1971; Meagher, 1979; Couger & Ishikawa, 1995; Brislin, 2005).

However, Herzberg"s theory was subject to some criticism. Some scholars criticized the notion that the motivators and hygienes are two independent factors, and that hygiene factors have no impact on motivating employees. They argued that some hygiene factors may act like motivators, and motivators can serve as sources of dissatisfaction and satisfaction.

2.2.1.3 ERG Theory

Clayton P. Alderfer (1972) is an American psychologist who extended and reformulated Maslow's theory. As a matter of fact, his theory can be considered as a variant of Maslow's theory. However, contradictory to Maslow, his theory was developed specifically for explaining work behavior in organizational settings (Steers, 2010).

Alderfer argued that the five need categories in Maslow's theory could be merged into three main categories, being "Existence", "Relatedness", and "Growth". Hence, the name of the theory (ERG) is adopted from the combination of the first letter of each need category (Hume, 2001).

The need of "Existence" refers to all forms of basic material and physiological needs required to maintain human existence. For example, the need for eating and drinking and other material needs in the work setting, like the need for pay, fringe benefits, and physical safety

(Schneider & Alderfer, 1973). "Relatedness" is the need for meaningful interpersonal relations in the work settings with superiors, peers, and subordinates.

However, the basic quality that distinguishes the relatedness needs from existence needs is that one cannot satisfy the relatedness apart from others, thus it cannot be satisfied without mutuality (Schneider & Alderfer, 1973). "Growth" needs are associated with the development of one's potential (Steers, 2010). Schneider and Alderfer (1973) argued that, "satisfaction of this category occurs when a person engages problems which call upon him to make the most of his capacities and to build up new capabilities".

Although the ERG theory may seem to have much in common with the work of Maslow, his work has some substantial differences. Alderfer agreed with Maslow that when people satisfy their lower needs, they tended to move up the hierarchy from "Existence" needs, to "Relatedness" needs, and finally to "Growth" needs. However, unlike Maslow's hierarchy, Alderfer argued that all different levels of needs may be activated and operated in a given person at the same time (Huczynski & Buchanan, 2001). Therefore, any category of needs can be activated without the condition of fulfilling the other needs. In other words, the individual can be motivated by his desire for money (an Existence need), interpersonal relations (a Relatedness need), and by recognition (a Growth need) simultaneously (Brooks, 2003). Accordingly, the order of the needs may differ from one person to another according to his preferences and own framework.

The flexibility of the ERG theory enables it to explain a wider range of human behavior. For example, why some people seek to satisfy their needs for achievement or recognition, or can achieve a high level of self-actualization although they may have a very low salary. Furthermore, Alderfer's ERG theory suggests that there is also a frustration-regression sequence, as when a higher level need remains unfulfilled and it appears difficult to be fulfilled, the individual may regress to lower level need which will drive his behaviour. For example, if an individual cannot satisfy his growth needs, frustration regression occurs, causing the individual to focus on fulfilling his relatedness or existence needs (Steers, 2010).

2.2.1.4 Relationships between Different Content Theories

Despite the differences between the need theories discussed above, there are several points at which the theories intersect. The table below illustrates the similarities among the three previous theories.

Type of motivation	Herzberg's Categories	Maslow's Categories	Alderfer's E-RG Categories
Intrinsic	Work itself Achievement Possibility of growth	Self-actualization	Growth
	Responsibility	Esteem-self-confirmed	
	Motivators Advancement	Esteem-interpersonal	
	Recognition		**Relatedness**
Extrinsic	Status	**Social needs**	
	Relation with supervisors Peer relations	**Safety**-interpersonal	
	Relations with subordinates		
	Company policies	**Safety**-material	
	Hygiene Job security		**Existence**
	Working conditions	**Physiological needs**	
	Pay		

Relationships among content motivation theories

By and large, despite the differences between the three content theories, Maslow's theory can be considered as the basis for the ERG theory, the difference between the two theories being the number of need categories. According to Schneider and Alderfer (1973) and Luthans (2000), the "Existence" needs in the ERG theory are equivalent to Maslow's physiological needs, and the part of the safety needs that are related to safety with material needs (physical threats), it is also equivalent to a part of Herzberg's hygiene factors.

Moreover, the "Relatedness" needs in the ERG theory are equivalent to Maslow's social needs and both the safety with interpersonal needs and the esteem that relies on the interaction with others; it is also equivalent to a part of both Herzberg's hygiene and motivators factors. On the other hand, the "Growth" needs in ERG theory are equivalent to Maslow's self-actualization needs and the esteem which relies on self-confirmed (one's internal standards); it is also equivalent to a part of Herzberg's motivators. Overall, although the need theories differ in determining the number of human needs and the relationships between these needs, they do agree in the fact that satisfying these needs is a basic pillar in motivating employees' behaviour (Greenberg & Baron, 2002).

However, the main deficiency of the content theories is that it cannot explain the complexity of human motivation process (Luthans, 2000).

2.2.2 Process Theories of Work Motivation

The major problem with the content theories is that it cannot explain the direction of the motivation process (Thompson and McHugh, 2002). On the other hand, the process theories have the ability to describe how behaviour is started and directed. Thus, it takes the dynamicity of the motivation process and the interaction between the variables involved into consideration (Analoui, 2000). Although there are various competent process theories, this section mainly focuses on two of the most prominent and widely known process theories of work motivation, namely Adam's Equity Theory (1965) and Vroom's Expectancy Theory (1964).

2.2.2.1 Equity Theory

The equity concept is a synonym of justice and fairness. This concept is usually used in the work context to express the positive association between one's efforts and performance, and the pay and other benefits one receives (Steers, 2010). The basic principle of equity theory that has been shared by different equity theorists is that rewards must be distributed among an organization's members according to their actual contribution, meaning that someone who contributes more should have more privileges than someone who contributes less (Deutsch, 2000).

Adams (1965) argued that "inequity occurs when a person thinks that the ratio of his outcomes to inputs and the ratio of other's outcomes to other's inputs are unequal".

Accordingly, the equity occurs when a person's outcomes to inputs = another's outcomes to inputs. On the other hand, there are two kinds of inequity. The first kind, "positive inequity", occurs when a person's outcomes to inputs > another's outcomes to inputs. The second kind of inequity, "negative inequity", can happen when a person's outcomes to inputs < another's outcomes to inputs (Adams, 1965). The inputs may include factors that an individual can give to his work such as qualifications, experience, hours, efforts, skills, loyalty, and devotion. On the other hand, outcomes represent what an individual can receive from his work, which may include pay, benefits, respect, security, prestige, pleasant work environment, promotions, and status. Moreover, both the person's inputs and outputs are mainly influenced by one's perceptions and expectations (Luthans, 2000).

Another point related to the Equity Theory is the reactions toward inequity. According to Adams, if a person perceived inequity he will try to bring the equity ratio into balance. Furthermore, people differ in their sensitivity toward equity, as Huseman (2010) stated that individuals come to terms with equity as one of three types:

Benevolents, those who prefer their outcome/input ratios to be less than the outcome/input ratios of the comparison other; "Equity Sensitizes", those who, conforming to the traditional norm of equity, prefer their outcome/input ratios to equal those of comparison others; and Entitleds, those who prefer their outcome/input ratios to exceed the comparison other's. (1987).

Also, the employee's position within the organization hierarchy has been found to be significant with sensitivity toward equity. As it has been found that managers perceived less inequity regarding pay, company policies, promotion, fringe benefits, advancement, and power than supervisors or workers (Singh, 2003).

2.2.2.2 Expectancy Theory

The Expectancy Theory derived its roots from the early work of Tolman and Honzik, (1930), who tried to produce a systematic explanatory theory of work motivation (Boorks, 2003). However, Vroom (1964) was the first who presented a systematic formulation of motivation that based on the expectancy assumptions developed for use in work situations (Steers, 2010). Since Vroom (1964) formulated what has been called the "Expectancy Theory", it has been widely used in managerial literature to explain the human behaviour within the workplace. Vroom refused the assumption of the content theories, that people have certain needs that they try to satisfy it, as he took the diversity and the complexity of the human behavior into consideration. Huczynski and Buchanan (2001) argued that the Expectancy Theory is more comprehensive than the content theories as it sheds light on the individual differences regarding motivation and behavior. Moreover, it helps us to measure the strength of an individual's motivation.

According to the theory, the human behaviour is determined by the preference and the possibility of getting the desired outcome.

2.3   Review of Empirical Literature

From the analysis of data collected, in a study on the Influence of planning and control on the organizational performance of agricultural state owned corporations by Precious Okere in (2015), planning was found to influence the performance of the agricultural state owned corporations in Nigeria by contributing in the following ways: improving on the time deliveries to the customers, improving on the standard of systems and technology, enhancing profitability, improving on the efficiency and growth, aligning resources to strategic initiatives, promoting customer satisfaction, ensuring that there is appropriate transfer of knowledge among employees, increasing on employee motivation and by ensuring appropriate sharing of knowledge among employees.

The influence of planning was also analyzed according to the four perspectives in the balance score model. The conclusions of these findings were that: in terms of financial perspective, strategic planning helps in reducing the operating costs. From the customers' perspective, planning and control helps improving on-time deliveries to customers, as well as enhancing on employee remuneration, hence increased motivation. On the learning and growth perspective, strategic planning and control ensures appropriate transfer of knowledge among employees and lastly on internal process perspective, planning for the corporation and control help in identifying risks and their mitigations as well as improving the standard of systems and technology (Richard, 2015)

From the findings both in literature and analysis of data, it was therefore concluded that planning and control are very important functions in the management of any organization and therefore, if the agricultural state owned corporations are to improve on their performance the managers must ensure that they effectively perform this function.

The work of Umuerure (2016) on Job satisfaction and motivation among senior and middle managers was considered. Job satisfaction is one of the most studied subjects in management literature because it is one of the most important human maintenance factors in any organization. The main concern of the study was to present and discuss the managerial literature regarding motivation and job satisfaction. The meaning of motivation and job satisfaction and the relationship between them were outlined. The different managerial schools of thought were presented, including the Traditional Model which adopted the classical Theory's ideas, which consider money as the only motivator, and that individuals can be motivated only by their desire for economic rewards.

However, in today's work environment the applications of its ideas are questionable as it was not concerned about the psychological or social needs of people in the workplace. The Human Relations Model was the second contributor to the motivation and job satisfaction development. It concentrated on the human aspects and the social relations between workers and encouraged the management to provide its employees with recognition and more autonomy. However, applying its principles may provide employees with a false sense of happiness as it is not actually concerned with their interests; moreover, it overemphasized on the human aspects on account of the interest of the organization as a whole.

The Human Resource Model was the third contributor to motivation researches as it provided the management and practitioners with two different approaches when dealing with subordinates, namely Theory X which has a negative and a pessimistic view about workers, and Theory Y, which has a positive and more optimistic view about workers.

Later, the main content motivation and job satisfaction theories were reviewed. Those theories were Maslow's Need Hierarchy, Herzeberg's Two Factor Theory, and Alderfer's ERG Theory. Each of these theories has focused on different dimensions of work motivation.

In addition, another research study considered the "impact of effective planning on Organizational Performance using Sterling bank Nigeria Plc as a case study by Olumuyiwa, (2012). However, the research study makes use of primary data of questionnaire analysis and the estimation technique adopted in the study was spearman's rank correlation coefficient and the objectives of the study was to determine the relationship between effective planning and organizational Performance and also to examine whether effective Planning leads to employees performance in an organization. In this study, the key issues that vie for managers time and attention is that of improving Performance; this is very important for both survival and maintenance of profit margins. Performance is a measure of how well resources are combined and utilized to accomplish specific desirable results to be able to achieve its objectives on organization need, articulate its strategies and carefully pursue them. There is no gain saying therefore that the success or otherwise of any organization depends on how effective their plans are.

According to him, the service industry offers intangible products; hence its efficiency and effectiveness can only be measured in terms of how well its services are delivered to its various publics. In recent years, the banking sector has witnessed tremendous growth. In fact, the sector is said to be the most active within the economy. Incidentally while the banking sector was booming there was recession in most other sectors of the economy. In other words, there was no commensurate growth. The completed deregulation of the banking sector made entry relatively easy (Olumuyiwa, 2012).

Similarly, the rate of collapse/demise also became high and this is traceable to poor environment analysis and lack of adequate planning on the part of the banks. The uncertainty inherent in the business environment makes it imperative that for any organization to succeed it must not only plan but vigorously implement and monitor such Plans (Olumuyiwa, 2012).

2.4   Theoretical Framework

2.4.1 Maslow's Hierarchy of Needs Theory

As discussed earlier, the Hierarchy of Needs Theory is considered one of the most famous theories in the field of human motivation and one of the first theories that attempt to describe the human behavior toward satisfying the different human needs (Kreitner, 2009). The theory is based on the assumption that a need affects a person's activities until he or she satisfies it (Steers *et al.*, 2010), thus the main motivator of people is their desire to satisfy their needs.

Maslow thought that personal needs can be arranged in a hierarchical order; in essence, once one of these needs has been satisfied, it will temporally lose its effect as a motivator and the person will focus on satisfying the next higher need which has been activated (Hilgert & Leonard, 2007; Luthans, 2000).

Steers (2010) demonstrated that, according to the Hierarchy Theory, people move from the bottom to the top of the need hierarchy through an active cycle of deprivation, domination, gratification and activation. As, when a person feels deprivation (unsatisfied need) in one of the hierarchy levels, this will direct his action toward satisfying this particular need. For example, if the person needs to satisfy his safety and security needs, he will temporarily ignore satisfying his higher-order needs; however, once he has met this need, the higher need will be activated and he will try to satisfy it, thus repeating this cycle of action until he reaches the apex of the need hierarchy. In this regard, Maslow categorizes the basic human needs into five levels in a hierarchy order, namely physiological needs, safety needs, social needs, esteem needs and self actualization needs, which can be illustrated in the following figure.

General Rewards	Need Levels	Organizational Factors
- Growth - Advancement - Creativity	**Self Actualization**	- Challenging job - Achievement in work - Advancement
- Self-esteem - Self-respect - Prestige	**Esteem Needs**	- Social recognition - Job title - High status job - Feedback
- Love - Affection - Belongingness	**Social Needs**	- Cohesive work group - Friendly supervision - Professional associations
- Safety - Security - Stability - Protection	**Safety Needs**	- Safe working conditions - Company benefits - Job security - Union - Pension
- Food - Water - Shelter - Sleep	**Physiological Needs**	- Pay - Good working conditions

Maslow's Hierarchy of Needs

The details of the five types of needs are as follows:

1   Physiological Needs: Maslow considered the physiological needs as the basis of the hierarchy. These needs are actually related to the different body and survival needs. For example, it included the need for eating, drinking, sleeping, and shelter. Maslow (1970) argued that these needs are the most dominant needs which the person will try to satisfy first; in the workplace, this level of needs reflects the employee's needs to have a suitable working environment (clean and fresh air, reasonable temperature, enough light and work-space) and good pay. According to Cherrington (2009), once these needs are satisfactorily met, it will lose its effect as a motivator and the safety needs (the second level in the hierarchy) will emerge and dominate the person's behavior.

2   Safety or Security Needs: These are related to the safety and security of the individual's physical and emotional conditions. Cherrington (2009), argued that when the individual feels the need for security, he or she becomes a safety-seeker and tries to satisfy it. This category of needs includes the desire for security, no threats or physical harm, and stability. In the workplace, this level of needs can be satisfied by providing job security (protection against layoff), safe working conditions (safe tools and environment), union, health insurance, and pension plans (Cherrington, 2009; Steers, 2010).

3   The Belongingness and Love Needs: Most people like to be a part of a group. Therefore, when the individual satisfies the two previous needs, the belongingness and love needs will emerge. This category of needs expresses the human needs for receiving love and to belong to a human group and be accepted by others. However, Luthans (2000) argued that Maslow's choice of the word "love" to address this category may have confusing connotations, such as sex, and it may be more appropriate to use the word "social needs" instead. The main ways to meet this kind of needs is through interaction as part of a work group, friendly supervision, professional associations, and a cohesive work group (Cherrington, 2009; Hilgert & Leonard, 2001).

4   **Esteem and Ego Needs:** This represents one of the higher human needs. It includes the needs for high power, high status, recognition for good work, achievement, self-respect, prestige, and attention from others. In the workplace, this level of needs can be met by sound job title, good feedback, and a high status job (Vecchio, 2000). Maslow argued that, "Satisfaction of the self-esteem need leads to feelings of self-confidence, worth, strength, capability and adequacy of being useful and necessary in the world.

5   **Self-Actualization Needs:** According to Maslow, self-actualization is what a man can be, he must be" and he considered it as the apex of the needs hierarchy. This kind of needs is actually an inner need for developing one's unique potential as an individual. In an organization, an employee may try to satisfy self-actualization needs by looking for challenging, innovative tasks or to make significant achievements to his job (Steers, 2010).

After Maslow had set his theory, some researchers made some changes in the format of the theory. For example, Porter (2006) in his study of middle and bottom managers added a new level that he called "autonomy" between the fourth level (esteem needs) and the fifth level (self-actualization needs). Porter claimed that needs such as those for authority, independent thought and participating in the setting of goals are logically distinct from more common esteem items Porter (2006). Another modification was made by Alderfer (1972), as he combined Maslow's physiological and safety needs into "Existence" (E) needs, belongingness and esteem needs into "Relatedness" (R) needs and the self-actualization need was renamed as "Growth" (G) need. Moreover, Lawler and Suttle (1972) offered another modification by reducing the five levels to just two levels; they called the first level the "physiological needs", and the second level they called the "higher needs", which contains Maslow's four other needs.

Maslow's theory is considered one of the most widely accepted theories in management context and is still very popular among researchers and practitioners (Soper, 2000). Bridwell (1976) argued that Maslow's hierarchy theory has proven to be a very useful theory in generating managerial ideas. Moreover, it is still popular among managers because it is very simple to present and easy to understand (Benson, 2003). It has inspired researchers over the past decades as it generated a number of management approaches and policies such as job enrichment, total quality management, business reengineering, self-managing teams, and employee empowerment (Huczynski & Buchanan, 2001). This theory relates to the impact of planning and control on organizational Performance for its rich managerial approaches for overall job performance. It can be said that when the step-by-step growth of any organization is considered, the Maslow's hierarchy of needs theory is a necessity for its employers-employees' relationship.

2.4.2 Expectancy Theory

Also, we earlier saw discussed that the Expectancy Theory derived its roots from the early work of Tolman and Honzik (1930), who tried to produce a systematic explanatory theory of work motivation (Boorks, 2003). However, Vroom (1964) was the first who presented a systematic formulation of motivation that based on the expectancy assumptions developed for use in work situations (Steers, 2010).

Since Vroom (1964) formulated what has been called the "Expectancy Theory", it has been widely used in managerial literature to explain the human behaviour within the workplace. Vroom refused the assumption of the content theories, that people have certain needs that they try to satisfy it, as he took the diversity and the complexity of the human behavior into consideration. Huczynski and Buchanan (2001) argued that the Expectancy Theory is more comprehensive than the content theories as it sheds light on the individual differences regarding motivation and behavior. Moreover, it helps us to measure the strength of an individual's motivation.

According to the theory, the human behaviour is determined by the preference and the possibility of getting the desired outcome. Accordingly, people will be motivated if they expect a positive relationship between efforts and rewards, and if they value these rewards. The basic elements of this theory are shown below;

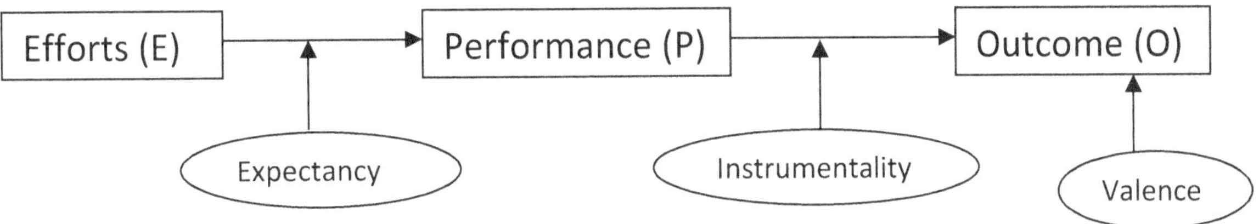

The basic elements of Expectancy Theory

Source: Huczynski and Buchanan (2001: 145)

As shown by the above figure, the Expectancy Theory comprises three elements. These elements are Expectancy, Instrumentality, and Valence.

Expectancy: According to Vroom's terminology, expectancy represents the employee's estimation of the relationship between effort and performance (E-P), and it is defined as an individual's subjective probability that changing in effort will lead to change in performance. In order to raise expectancy, the individual must have the required ability, experience, tools, and the appropriate opportunity to perform (Samson & Daft, 2002). Kreitner (2001) have pointed to the factors that influence an employee's expectancy perceptions. These are:

• Self-esteem

• Self-efficacy

• Previous experience and success at the assigned task

• Receiving the required help from subordinates and superiors

• Having the required information to accomplish the task

• Fine materials and tools should be available.

Instrumentality: Instrumentality refers to the relationship between performance and results, and it is defined as an individual's subjective probability that a particular performance (P) will lead to particular outcomes (O). It can range from -1.0 to 1.0. An instrumentality of 1.0 means a complete relationship between performance and outcomes, and that the attainment of a particular outcome completely depends on job performance. An instrumentality of zero indicates no relationship between performance and outcome, and an instrumentality of -1.0 reveals a complete negative relationship between performance and outcomes, as high performance reduces the chance of getting the desired outcome (Kreitner, 2001).

Valence: Valence refers to the attractiveness of the anticipated outcomes (Yoder and Henneman, 1975). It can range from -1.0 to 1.0, whereas a valence of 1.0 means a very desirable outcome, zero valences is not an attractive outcome, and -1.0 means a very undesirable outcome, such as being fired. Outcomes refer to different anticipated consequences that may result from an individual's performance, such as pay, recognition, fringe benefits, acceptance by others, promotion and fatigue (Pinder, 2005).

According to Vroom, the absence of any of the previous three elements will lead to the absence of an individual's motivation. For instance, if an employee believes that he will not be promoted despite the amount of effort he gives in performing his job, he may reduce his efforts or may not be motivated at all (Smith, 2004).

The Expectancy Theory was modified by the work of Porter and Lawler (1968), who developed an expectancy model of motivation that refined and extended Vroom's work. This model attempted to recognize the source of individual's valences and expectancies and to link an individual's effort with his performance and job satisfaction (Kreitner, 2001).

According to Porter and Lawler (1968), there are two determinants of one's effort. First, the rewards one receives as a result of accomplishing his job, including both extrinsic (tangible) rewards such as pay and fringe benefits, or intrinsic (intangible) rewards such as recognition and a feeling of achievement. As if an individual feels a positive relationship between his efforts and getting the desired rewards, this in turn forms the expectancy and instrumentality elements of Vroom's theory. Second, the received rewards and the desire of these rewards (the value of these rewards). These two factors are combined together and form the valence element of Vroom's theory (Elding, 2006).

Overall, according to Lewis *et al.* (2005), Vroom's Expectancy Theory is a comprehensive theory that helps to forecast or explain task-related effort, and it enables us to understand the differences in an individual's motivation and helps in measuring these differences. Ferris (2000) argued that it can be considered as the most promising conceptualization of an employee's motivation. Vroom's Expectancy Theory was supported by the work of some other researchers, (Kominis & Emmanuel, 2007). Additionally, De-Klerk (2005) reported a moderate-strong empirical support and a strong industrial applicability for the expectancy theory.

Nevertheless, the Expectancy Theory has been criticized for many reasons. Luthans (2000) has criticized the theory by pointing out that "the expectancy model attempts only to mirror the complex motivational process; it does not attempt to describe how motivational decisions are actually made or to solve actual motivational problems facing a manager". Moreover, Buchanan, (2004) summarized the main criticism of the expectancy theory on the following grounds. First, the theory covers a range of interrelated variables and is complex and difficult to test. Second, the assumption that we make decisions using such a detailed calculus is questionable. Third, the impacts of coercion and job insecurity on performance are overlooked. Finally, the tests of the theory rely on being able to measure and correlate all those variables, using instruments and statistical methods.

CHAPTER THREE

METHODOLOGY

3.1   Research Design

Obi (2003) defined research design as "the basic plan which guides the data collection and analysis phases of a research project". It is the framework which specifies the type of information to be collected and sources of data collection procedure. The design employed in this research work is a descriptive survey method. It is important to determine the method and procedure adopted in this research work since it gives the reader background information on the impact of planning and control on organizational Performance.

3.2   Population of the Study

Population is the totality of any group, persons or objects which is defined by some unique attributes. That is to say that population is any group of being the researcher has focused attention on and chosen as approved topic of study. Based on this study, the population is 550 staff of 7Up Bottling Company Plc. This number cuts across all departments in the organization.

3.3   Sample and Sampling Techniques

Sampling is a process of selecting a given number or any portion of that population, for purpose of obtaining information for generalizing about the large population. Sampling technique is used to avoid possible errors in dealing with population. The population size was narrowed down to determine the sample size.

The statistical formula used in determining the sample size for this study is called the 'Taro Yamen's Formula'. Yamen provides a simplified formula to calculate sample sizes for proportions of infinite population. We know the population size, but do not know the variability in the proportion and cannot estimate the variability with maximum precision. Thus, the formula is given as:

$$N = \frac{N}{1+n(e)^2}$$

Where   n   =   sample size

N   =   total population size

1   =   constant

e   =   the assumed error margin or tolerable errors, which is taken as 5%

$$N = \frac{N}{1+n(e)^2}$$

$$N = 550 \text{ and } (e)^2 = (0.05)^2 = 0.0025$$

$$N = \frac{550}{1+550\,(0.0025)}$$

$$N = \frac{550}{2.375} = 231.57$$

$$n = 232$$

Therefore, the sample size for this study is 232.

3.4   Methods of Data Collection

The method of data collection used by the researcher for this project work is from both primary and secondary sources of data. The primary data used for this research work was gotten from structured questionnaires administered to relevant staff of 7Up Bottling

Company Plc, Aba. The purpose was to get their personal views on a number of issues. Questionnaire is used when the factual information is needed.

The Questionnaire used for this research work has multiple opinions for the questions, where respondents were provided with opinion of answers to choose only the right answer to their opinion. A Likert Scale ranging from 1-5 (1) strongly agree SA, (2) agree A, (3) undecided UD, (4) disagree DA, (5) strongly disagree SD was adopted for the questionnaire response. This form of research plan was chosen in order to ease the work of the researcher in the areas of classifying and analyzing individuals (respondents) opinions. The secondary sources from which data was collected include; textbooks, recent related research works as well as different websites on the internet.

3.5 Measurement of Variables

In order to ensure that a meaningful analysis was carried out for the purpose of providing clarity in understanding, an operational definition of the variables in this study is given. This will help to indicate the meaning of the variables, as it is functionally applied in the study and how numerical values were assigned to them. Measurement is the assignment of numbers to events or objects according to rules that permit important properties of the objects or events to be represented by properties of the number system.

Independent Variable Planning and control will be measured using contingency planning, tactical planning, operational control, and human and machine control. Many researchers have used these dimensions to measure this variable and were proven valid. The response to each of the items will be rated using a five point likert's scale labeled as follows: Strongly Agree (SA), Agree (A), Neutral (N). Disagree (D) and Strongly Disagree (SD) with a corresponding value of 5,4,3,2 and 1 through available information from 7up bottling company.

Dependent Variable: Organizational Performance is measured using effectiveness and efficiency. The response to each of the items will be rated using a five point likert's scale labeled as follows: Strongly Agree (SA), Agree (A), Neutral (N). Disagree (D) and Strongly Disagree (SD) with a corresponding value of 5,4,3,2 and 1 through available information from 7up bottling company.

3.6   Reliability and Validity of Research Instrument

Reliability: The research work is reliable for the fact that it was supervised by a more competent professional and reviews of related literature by earlier researchers were made. Besides, known methods of data analysis, Multiple Regression was also used to analyze the data gotten.

Validity: After the construction of the instrument, it was taken to my supervisor, who is a more competent professional for proper face and content validation, and he made the necessary corrections and additions. The instrument was also taken to other statistical/research experts who made their contributions and approval.

3.7   Methods of Data Analysis

According to Ogomaka (2011), the Mathematical and statistical methods employed in the analysis and interpretation of the outcome of research instrument with respect to hypothesis is data analysis. Analysis of the gathered data as regards this study is based on Multiple Regression Analysis.

The researcher intends to use Multiple Linear Regression on Qualitative Variates. The choice of Multiple Linear Regression analysis is that, its analysis compiled observations of people's attitudes or opinions derived from a questionnaire, polling, or measurement of some kind of subjective evaluations.

3.8   Limitation of the Study

In every research effort, there must be some constraints or limiting factors. The constraints or limiting factors in course of this research work include:

Time: The researcher did not have enough time to carry out the research, especially following the outbreak of the Corona Virus (COVID-19) pandemic, and this posed a problem to the researcher and even to the research work. Also, the pressure of other academic obligations and commitments of the researcher made it difficult for the researcher to carry out her research work effectively.

Finance: Financial problem is another limiting factor to every research work. Given the incessant requirements like in prices of goods and services, including textbooks and most especially, in transportation, the researcher found it very challenging to visit places of relevance such as libraries, companies, banking sectors and so on.

However, despite these limitations, the researcher was of the view that the imminent obstacles would be managed with the hope of achieving optimum results. The researcher overcame the above challenges through the help of family and friends.

CHAPTER FOUR

DATA PRESENTATION, ANALYSIS AND DISCUSSION OF FINDINGS

4.1 Characteristics of the Sample

Table 4.1: Analysis of Respondents Profile

S/N	Variables	Frequency	Percentage (%)
1	Gender:		
	Male	112	48
	Female	120	52
	Total	232	100
2	Age Range:		
	18- 25years	38	16.3
	26-35years	86	37
	36-45years	63	28
	46 years and above	45	19
	Total	232	100
3	Marital Status:		
	Single	99	43
	Married	125	54
	Divorced	8	3
	Total	232	100
4	Educational Qualification		
	School Certificate	32	14
	OND/NCE	60	26
	HND/B.Sc	116	50
	Master/PhD	24	10
	Total	232	100
5	Years of Job Experience:		
	Below 5years	98	42
	5-10years	95	41
	11 years and above	39	17
	Total	232	100

Source: Field Survey, 2021

Table 4.1 exhibits the background characteristics of the various respondents. The gender of the respondents showed that 48% of the samples were males, while 52% were females. The age bracket of the respondents indicates that 16% of the respondents were below 25 years of age; 37% of the respondents' falls within the age bracket of 26-35 years of age, 28% of the respondents' falls within the age bracket of 36-45 years of age while 19% of the respondents were 46 years of age and above. The marital composition of the respondents indicated that; 43% of the respondents were single, 54% of the respondents were married, while 3% of the other respondents were divorced. On the educational background of the sample, it was indicated that 14% of the respondents were SSCE holders, 26% of the respondents were OND/NCE holders, 50% of the respondents were HND/B.Sc holders, while 10% of the other respondents were Master/Ph.D degree holders. On the years of work experience, 42% of the respondents had below 5years working experience, 41% of the respondents had within 5-10years working experience, while 17% of the respondents had above 11 years working experience.

4.2   Data Presentation

Table 4.2 Analysis from the Field Survey

Pattern focused	Number administered	Number returned	Number used
Employees	232	232	232

Source: Distributed Questionnaire

The 232 copies of questionnaire administered and retrieved were properly filled. Therefore, the analysis in this chapter was based on the response rate of 100%.

4.3 Descriptive Analysis

This section focused on the analyses of responses to the main research questions using the 5 point Likert scale. They were analyzed using correlation and multiple regression analysis.

Table 4.3.1 Correlation Analyses of the Dimensions of Planning and Control

S/N	Dimensions of planning and control	Mean	Std. Deviation	N	1	2	3	4	5
1	Contingency planning	18.55	1.39	232	1				
2	Tactical planning	18.41	1.56	232	.698**	1			
3	Operational control	18.73	1.45	232	.657**	.688**	1		
4	Human and machine control	18.77	1.43	232	.747**	.554**	.767**	1	
5	Organizational Performance	18.75	1.44	232	.809**	.635**	.655**	.836**	1

**. Correlation is significant at the 0.01 level (2-tailed).

Table 4.3.1 showed that all the correlation coefficients between the constructs in this study showed high positive correlation.

The correlation coefficient between contingency planning and organizational Performance showed strong positive relationship (r = 0.809**, p < .01).

Tactical planning which is the second variable exhibited strong positive correlation with organizational Performance (r = 0.635**, p < .01).

Operational control which is the third variable exhibited strong positive correlation with organizational Performance (r = 0.655**, p < .01).

Human and machine control which is the last variable has strong positive correlation with organizational Performance (r = 0.836**, p < .01).

Table 4.3.2: Multiple Regression analysis of planning and control and organizational Performance

Coefficients[a]

Model		Unstandardized Coefficients		Standardized Coefficients		
		B	Std. Error	Beta	t	Sig.
1	(Constant)	.699	.650		1.076	.283
	Contingency planning	.353	.056	.341	6.332	.000
	Tactical planning	.148	.045	.160	3.302	.001
	Operational control	-.136	.055	-.137	-2.497	.013
	Human and machine control	.604	.057	.597	10.548	.000

a. Dependent Variable: Organizational Performance

Table 4.4 showed the multiple regression analysis result for the effects of all the dimensions of planning and control on organizational Performance. It was indicated that contingency planning which was the first variable has positive effect on organizational Performance (ß = 0.341, P<0.05). Tactical planning which is the second variable has positive effect on organizational Performance (ß = 0.160, P<0.05). It was indicated that operational control which is the third variable has negative effect on organizational Performance (ß = -0.137, P<0.05). It was also shown that human and machine control which is the last variable has a higher positive effect on organizational Performance (ß = 0.597, P<0.05).

The general form of the equation to predict OP = $\beta_o + \beta_1 CP + \beta_2 TP + \beta_3 OC + \beta_4 HMC + \varepsilon$

MP = .699 + (0.353×CP) + (0.148×TP) + (-0.136×OC) + (0.604×HMC)

Table 4.3.3 Analysis of Variance

ANOVA[a]

Model		Sum of Squares	Df	Mean Square	F	Sig.
1	Regression	377.276	4	94.319	209.446	.000[b]
	Residual	102.224	227	.450		
	Total	479.500	231			

a. Dependent Variable: Organizational Performance
b. Predictors: (Constant), Human and machine control , Tactical planning , Contingency planning , Operational control

The F-ratio in table 4.5 tests, showed that the sub independent variables (human and machine control, tactical planning, contingency planning, operational control) statistically predict the dependent variable (organizational Performance), $F = 209.446$, $p < 0.05$. This showed that the regression model is a good fit of the data.

Table 4.3.4: Model Summary

Model Summary

Model	R	R Square	Adjusted R Square	Std. Error of the Estimate
1	.887[a]	.787	.783	.6711

a. Predictors: (Constant), Human and machine control , Tactical planning , Contingency planning , Operational control

Table 4.6 indicated that change in organizational Performance was brought about by the dimensions of planning and control by 78% (0.783) as indicated by the adjusted R^2 value. The dimensions of planning and control (i.e human and machine control, tactical planning, contingency planning, operational control) explained 78% of the variability of organizational Performance.

4.4 Tests of Hypotheses

The multiple regression analysis was used as an analytical technique for testing the hypotheses of the study.

Decision Rule

If the probability value calculated is greater than the critical level of significance, then the null hypothesis is accepted and the alternate hypothesis is rejected. The P-value is the lowest significant level at which a null hypothesis can be rejected (Gujarati & Porter, 2009). Therefore, the P-value = 0.05(5%).

H_{O1} There is no significant relationship between contingency planning and organizational Performance.

Since the P value calculated in Table 4.4 is lesser than the critical level of significance (0.000 < 0.05), the null hypothesis was rejected while the alternate hypothesis was accepted this implies that there is a significant relationship between contingency planning and organizational Performance.

H_{O2}: There is no significant relationship between tactical planning and organizational Performance.

Since the p value calculated in Table 4.4 is lesser than the critical level of significance (0.001 < 0.05), there was need to reject the null hypothesis and accept the alternate hypothesis indicating that there is a significant relationship between tactical planning and organizational Performance.

H_{O3}: There is no significant relationship between operational control and organizational Performance.

The P value calculated in Table 4.4 is lesser than the critical level of significance (0.013 < 0.05), therefore the null hypothesis was rejected while the alternate hypothesis was accepted implying that there is a significant relationship between operational control and organizational Performance.

H$_{O4}$: There is no significant relationship between human and machine control and organizational Performance. Since the P value calculated in table 4.4 is lesser than the critical level of significance (0.000 < 0.05). The null hypothesis was rejected while the alternate hypothesis was accepted, this implies that there is a significant relationship between human and machine control and organizational Performance.

4.5 Discussion of Findings

In line with the findings from the study analyses, as well as the review of relevant literatures, the findings of this study are presented as follows.

4.5.1 Contingency Planning and Organizational Performance

Table 4.3 showed that the correlation coefficient between contingency planning and organizational Performance showed strong positive relationship (r = 0.809**, p < .01). Table 4.5 indicated that contingency planning which was the first variable has positive effect on organizational Performance (ß = 0.341, P<0.05). H$_1$ result showed that there is a significant relationship between contingency planning and organizational Performance (0.000 < 0.05). Contingency planning involves planning what a business will do if something goes wrong, such as a failure of the original business plan, a lawsuit or an emergency situation caused by a natural disaster.

4.5.2 Tactical Planning Exhibited and Organizational Performance

Table 4.3 showed that tactical planning exhibited strong positive correlation with organizational Performance (r = 0.635**, p < .01). Table 4.5 indicated that tactical planning which is the second variable has positive effect on organizational Performance (ß = 0.160, P<0.05). H$_2$ result showed that there is a significant relationship between tactical planning and organizational Performance (0.001 < 0.05). Tactical planning involves determining the steps a business must take to reach the objectives developed through strategic planning.

Tactical plans will inevitably change as your strategic goals and aspects of the business context change.

4.5.3 Operational Control and Organizational Performance

Table 4.3 showed that operational control exhibited strong positive correlation with organizational Performance ($r = 0.655^{**}$, $p < .01$). Table 4.4 indicated that operational control which is the third variable has negative effect on organizational Performance ($ß = -0.137$, $P < 0.05$). H_3 result showed that there is a significant relationship between operational control and organizational Performance ($0.013 < 0.05$). Organizational and operational control serves to regulate the day-to-day output relative to schedules, specifications, and costs. Organizational control tends to review and evaluate the nature and arrangement of components in the system, whereas operational control tends to adjust the daily inputs (Nnenna, 2002).

4.5.4 Human/Machine Control and Organizational Performance

Table 4.3 showed that human and machine control has strong positive correlation with organizational Performance ($r = 0.836^{**}$, $p < .01$). Table 4.4 showed that human and machine control which is the last variable has a higher positive effect on organizational Performance ($ß = 0.597$, $P < 0.05$). H_4 result showed that there is a significant relationship between human and machine control and organizational performance ($0.000 < 0.05$). Most organized systems are some combination of man and machine; some elements of control are performed by machine whereas others are accomplished by man.

CHAPTER FIVE

SUMMARY OF FINDINGS, CONCLUSION AND RECOMMENDATIONS

5.1 Summary of Findings

Finding showed that the dimensions of planning and control (human and machine control, tactical planning, contingency planning, operational control) explained 78% of the variability of organizational Performance.

Finding indicated that contingency planning has positive effect on organizational Performance (β = 0.341, P<0.05). H_1 showed that there is a significant relationship between contingency planning and organizational performance (0.000 < 0.05).

Finding indicated that tactical planning has positive effect on organizational Performance (β = 0.160, P<0.05). H_2 showed that there is a significant relationship between tactical planning and organizational performance (0.001 < 0.05).

Finding indicated that operational control has negative effect on organizational Performance (β = -0.137, P<0.05). H_3 showed that there is a significant relationship between operational control and organizational Performance (0.013 < 0.05).

Finding showed that human and machine control has a higher positive effect on organizational Performance (β = 0.597, P<0.05). H_4 showed that there is a significant relationship between human and machine control and organizational Performance (0.000 < 0.05).

5.2 Conclusion

The study concluded that planning and control has positive significant effect on organizational Performance. Human and machine control, tactical planning, contingency planning, operational control has positive significant relationship with organizational Performance. Planning and controlling involve the plan or pattern of act that adds company main goals, policies and action systems unified into a whole. Planning and controlling

methods empower managers to convert data into valued decisions and appropriate actions. .
The planning and controlling process also creates timelines for when the plans should be
achieved.

5.3 Recommendations

i. Plans should be simple to understand and not ambiguous because complexity of plans leads to confusion and impossibility of accomplishment.

ii. A good plan that is expected to expand profit should be based on the information collected and such information must be stated in the plan for future review.

iii. For any organization to be productive, managers or planners should have a number of different contingency plans to address emergency situations that could arise, as each may require a different course of action.

iv. Tactical plans are meant to increase probability that the organization will achieve its objectives. This follows therefore that steps in tactical plans should not be violated.

v. Human and machine control, being one of the most important components which gear toward organizational Performance, should often be considered from the start-up of the organization.

REFERENCES

Abdalkrim, G.M. (2013). The impact of strategic planning activities on private sector organizations performance in Sudan: An empirical research. *International Journal of Business and Management*, 8(10), 134.

Adongo, K.O., & Jagongo, A. (2013). Budgetary control as a measure of financial performance of state corporations in Kenya. *International Journal of Accounting and Taxation*, 1(1).

Akinyele, S.T., & Fasogbon, O.I. (2010). Impact of strategic planning on organizational performance and survival. *Research Journal of Business Management*, 4(1), 73-82.

Al Khattab, S. A., & Aldehayyat, J.S. (2011). Perceptions of service quality in Jordanian hotels. *International Journal of Business and Management*, 6(7), 226.

Alalade, S.Y., & Oguntodu, J.A. (2015). Motivation and employees' performance in the Nigerian banking industry.

Amara, T.C, (2002). Quantitative techniques business, Aba: Matic Publisher

Awai. D & Owede K (2012). Techniques in educational research.

Chima, O. (2000). Fundamentals of business management in Nigeria, second edition.

Dawson, L. (2013). Analysing planning in an organization, *Journal of Management Science*, University of London, Macmillan press, Lagos.

Aham, A. (2000). Dimensions of Marketing. Klet Ken Publishers, Owerri

Dixon G. (2011). Planning and management organization, Sweden business school publication Wiley and sons press limited, New York.

Drucker, P.F. (2003). The theory and practice of management, a broader perspective, 4th edition, 98-114, New York Press

Drucker, P.F (2004). Management, task, responsibilities and practices, a textbook 3rd edition, 45-63, New York harper and row publication limited.

Felistus Chepchirchir Kabiru, (2018): The influence of planning on the organizational performance of agricultural state owned corporations in Kenya

Ferris, K.R. (2000). Perceived environmental uncertainty, organizational adaptation, and employee performance: A longitudinal study in professional accounting firms. *Accounting Organizations and Society*, 7(1), 13-25.

Frucot, V. & Shearon, W. T. (2010). Budgetary participation, focus of control, and Mexican managerial performance and job satisfaction. *The Accounting Review*, 80-98.

Geotz, N. (1999). Management and Planning, a propeller for organizational performance, *Journal of College of Management Goteburg University*, 11, 23-34, Plymouth Macdonald and even publication limited.

Koontz, H. O'Donnell, C., & Weibrich, H. (2000). Management in broader perspective, management of multidisciplinary study, Tokyo Macgraw hill publication limited.

Lookman B. F. (2011). The joint effect of task characteristics and organizational context on job performance

Luthans, F. (2017). Successful and effective real management, the academy of management executive, 88-89

Mitchell, T. R., Holtom, B. C., & Lee, T. W. (2001). How to keep your best employees: Developing an effective retention policy. *Academy of Management Executive*, 15(4), 96-103.

Nnena B.A. (2000). Principles of management: Lyke ventures, Enugu.

Nwachukwu, C. (2011). Management theory and practice, Owerri African publication

Obi, E.C. (2000). The concept and practice of management: Global Prints, Aba.

Ogomaka, P.M.C (2011). Descriptive educational statistics: A guide to research. Owerri Totan.

Ojemba, G.A. (2000). Principles of Management. Lyke venutes, Enugu

Parkinson, C.N. (2000). Impact of planning on organizational performance, *Journal of Social Science,* 5, 99-1233, Parkinsonis law, Boston, Houghton Mifflin publication limited.

Samuel, O. (2012). Effective planning and organizational performance. (A case study of Sterling Bank Nigeria Plc).

Schermerhorn, J. (2011). Management for performance, a textbook 2nd edition, 76-89. New York, John wile and sons publication limited.

Schermerhorn, J. (2009). Management and organizational behaviour, 2nd edition, 227-36, New York, Wiley and sons publication limited.

Stoner, J. (2000). Management and planning, a broader perspective, a textbook, 2nd edition, New Jersey, Prentice hall publication limited.

QUESTIONNAIRE

Department of Business Administration,

Faculty of Management Science,

Federal University Otuoke,

Bayelsa State.

Dear respondent,

I am an undergraduate student of the above named institution. I am conducting a research on the "Effect of planning and control on organizational Performance in 7up bottling company, Aba branch". The questionnaire is designed to elicit your opinion on how planning and control will affect organizational Performance. This exercise is strictly academic and your view will be treated with confidence. It shall be appreciated if you will kindly respond objectively to the questions in the structured questionnaire. Names are not required, therefore confidentiality is guaranteed.

Thanks for your anticipated cooperation

Joseph Azibagiri

(***Researcher***)

QUESTIONNAIRE

PLANNING AND CONTROL QUESTIONNAIRE

Please complete the following and tick in the current boxes

SECTION A: PERSONAL DATA

1. Gender: Male ☐   Female ☐

2. Marital status: (a) single ☐   (b) married ☐   (c) divorced ☐

3. Your qualification: (a) O'Level ☐   (b) HND ☐   (c) BSc ☐   (d) M.Sc ☐   (e) Ph.D ☐

4. Age: (a) 15-25 ☐   (b) 26-30 ☐   (c) 31-40 ☐   (d) 40-50 ☐

5. Work experience: Less than 1yr ☐   1-5yr ☐   6-10yrs ☐   11-20yrs ☐

   Above 20yrs ☐

SECTION B

A Likert Scale ranging from 1-5 (1) strongly agree SA, (2) agree A, (3) undecided UD, (4) disagree DA, (5) strongly disagree SD is going to be adopted in this section

RESEARCH QUESTION ONE; Does contingency planning influence organizational Performance?

S/N		SA	A	UD	DA	SD
		1	2	3	4	5
6	Management and Employees are ready to take action should an emergency occur					
7	Each regulated entity properly trained employees on contingency plan					
8	My organization identified materials and resources for use during an emergency within the organization					
9	My organization identify common emergencies that could occur at each facility in the organization					

RESEARCH QUESTION TWO: To what extent does tactical planning affect organizational Performance?

S/N		SA 1	A 2	UD 3	DA 4	SD 5
10	Resources allocated to each department for day to day operations are effectively utilized by designated managers					
11	The steps to take in attainment of my departmental goals are clearly spelt out					
12	My organization established cordial relationship with our customers					
13	Departmental goals are in tandem with the organizational goals					

RESEARCH QUESTIONS THREE: What is the influence of operational control on organizational Performance?

S/N		SA 1	A 2	UD 3	DA 4	SD 5
14	My organization measure Performance or output of individuals and teams					
15	My organization have a well-defined written production process					
16	My organization provide incentive for operations staff to achieve their targets					
17	My organization have quality control processes in place					

RESEARCH QUESTION FOUR: Does human and machine control influence organizational Performance?

S/N		SA	A	UD	DA	SD
		1	2	3	4	5
18	My organization have effective system for monitoring employees activities in work environment					
19	Employees punctuality at work is paramount to the managers of individual departments					
20	My organization ensures that machines are not over utilized before servicing					
21	Machines in my organization are operated by qualified personnel					

SECTION C

A Likert Scale ranging from 1-5 (1) strongly agree SA, (2) agree A, (3) undecided UD, (4) disagree DA, (5) strongly disagree SD is going to be adopted in this section

S/N		SA	A	UD	DA	SD
		1	2	3	4	5
22	Through effective planning programs my organization develop superior quality assurance mechanisms					
23	Performance in 7up could be rated high					
24	Effective planning and control has improved Performance in my organization					
25	Effective planning and control lead to increased customer base					

```
DATASET ACTIVATE DataSet6.
GET DATA /TYPE=XLSX
  /FILE='C:\Users\HP\Documents\Faith Data.xlsx'
  /SHEET=name 'Sheet1'
  /CELLRANGE=full
  /READNAMES=on
  /ASSUMEDSTRWIDTH=32767.
EXECUTE.
DATASET NAME DataSet9 WINDOW=FRONT.
REGRESSION
  /MISSING LISTWISE
  /STATISTICS COEFF OUTS R ANOVA
  /CRITERIA=PIN(.05) POUT(.10)
  /NOORIGIN
  /DEPENDENT OrganizationalPerformance
  /METHOD=ENTER Contingencyplanning Tacticalplanning Operationalcontrol
Humanandmachinecontrol.
```

Regression

Notes

Output Created		21-JUL-2021 08:39:55
Comments		
Input	Active Dataset	DataSet9
	Filter	<none>
	Weight	<none>
	Split File	<none>
	N of Rows in Working Data File	232
Missing Value Handling	Definition of Missing	User-defined missing values are treated as missing.
	Cases Used	Statistics are based on cases with no missing values for any variable used.

Syntax		REGRESSION
		  /MISSING LISTWISE
		  /STATISTICS COEFF OUTS R ANOVA
		  /CRITERIA=PIN(.05) POUT(.10)
		  /NOORIGIN
		  /DEPENDENT OrganizationalPerformance
		  /METHOD=ENTER Contingencyplanning Tacticalplanning Operationalcontrol Humanandmachinecontrol.

Resources	Processor Time	00:00:00.08
	Elapsed Time	00:00:00.14
	Memory Required	2692 bytes
	Additional Memory Required for Residual Plots	0 bytes

Variables Entered/Removed[a]

Model	Variables Entered	Variables Removed	Method
1	Human and machine control , Tactical planning , Contingency planning , Operational control[b]	.	Enter

a. Dependent Variable: Organizational Performance

b. All requested variables entered.

Model Summary

Model	R	R Square	Adjusted R Square	Std. Error of the Estimate
1	.887[a]	.787	.783	.6711

a. Predictors: (Constant), Human and machine control , Tactical planning ,

Contingency planning , Operational control

ANOVA[a]

Model		Sum of Squares	df	Mean Square	F	Sig.
1	Regression	377.276	4	94.319	209.446	.000[b]
	Residual	102.224	227	.450		
	Total	479.500	231			

a. Dependent Variable: Organizational Performance

b. Predictors: (Constant), Human and machine control , Tactical planning , Contingency planning ,

Operational control

Coefficients[a]

Model		Unstandardized Coefficients		Standardized Coefficients	t	Sig.
		B	Std. Error	Beta		
1	(Constant)	.699	.650		1.076	.283
	Contingency planning	.353	.056	.341	6.332	.000
	Tactical planning	.148	.045	.160	3.302	.001
	Operational control	-.136	.055	-.137	-2.497	.013
	Human and machine control	.604	.057	.597	10.548	.000

a. Dependent Variable: Organizational Performance

```
CORRELATIONS

  /VARIABLES=Contingencyplanning Tacticalplanning Operationalcontrol

Humanandmachinecontrol

    OrganizationalPerformance

  /PRINT=TWOTAIL NOSIG

  /STATISTICS DESCRIPTIVES

  /MISSING=PAIRWISE.
```

Correlations

Notes

Output Created		21-JUL-2021 08:40:50
Comments		
Input	Active Dataset	DataSet9
	Filter	<none>
	Weight	<none>
	Split File	<none>
	N of Rows in Working Data File	232
Missing Value Handling	Definition of Missing	User-defined missing values are treated as missing.
	Cases Used	Statistics for each pair of variables are based on all the cases with valid data for that pair.

Syntax		CORRELATIONS
		  /VARIABLES=Contingencyplanning Tacticalplanning Operationalcontrol Humanandmachinecontrol
		    OrganizationalPerformance
		  /PRINT=TWOTAIL NOSIG
		  /STATISTICS DESCRIPTIVES
		  /MISSING=PAIRWISE.

Resources	Processor Time	00:00:00.09
	Elapsed Time	00:00:00.11

Descriptive Statistics

	Mean	Std. Deviation	N
Contingency planning	18.547	1.3918	232
Tactical planning	18.414	1.5574	232
Operational control	18.728	1.4503	232
Human and machine control	18.767	1.4255	232
Organizational Performance	18.750	1.4407	232

Correlations

		Contingency planning	Tactical planning	Operational control	Human and machine control	Organizational Performance
Contingency planning	Pearson Correlation	1	.698**	.657**	.747**	.809**
	Sig. (2-tailed)		.000	.000	.000	.000
	N	232	232	232	232	232
Tactical planning	Pearson Correlation	.698**	1	.688**	.554**	.635**
	Sig. (2-tailed)	.000		.000	.000	.000
	N	232	232	232	232	232
Operational control	Pearson Correlation	.657**	.688**	1	.767**	.655**
	Sig. (2-tailed)	.000	.000		.000	.000
	N	232	232	232	232	232
Human and machine control	Pearson Correlation	.747**	.554**	.767**	1	.836**
	Sig. (2-tailed)	.000	.000	.000		.000
	N	232	232	232	232	232
Organizational Performance	Pearson Correlation	.809**	.635**	.655**	.836**	1
	Sig. (2-tailed)	.000	.000	.000	.000	
	N	232	232	232	232	232

**. Correlation is significant at the 0.01 level (2-tailed).